Miller Analogies Test (MAT) DVD from Trivium Test Prep!

Dear Customer,

Thank you for purchasing from Trivium Test Prep! We're honored to help you prepare for your AP exam.

To show our appreciation, we're offering a **FREE *MAT Essential Test Tips* DVD by Trivium Test Prep**. Our DVD includes 35 test preparation strategies that will make you successful on the AP Exam. All we ask is that you email us your feedback and describe your experience with our product. Amazing, awful, or just so-so: we want to hear what you have to say!

To receive your **FREE *MAT Essential Test Tips* DVD**, please email us at 5star@triviumtestprep.com. Include "Free 5 Star" in the subject line and the following information in your email:

1. The title of the product you purchased.

2. Your rating from 1 – 5 (with 5 being the best).

3. Your feedback about the product, including how our materials helped you meet your goals and ways in which we can improve our products.

4. Your full name and shipping address so we can send your **FREE *MAT Essential Test Tips* DVD**.

If you have any questions or concerns please feel free to contact us directly at 5star@triviumtestprep.com. Thank you!

- Trivium Test Prep Team

Table of Contents

Introduction

An Overview of the MAT

The Miller Analogies Test (MAT) is an examination that is used by many graduate schools to assess potential students' content knowledge and analytical reasoning. This is done through the use of analogies – problems stated as relationships.

An analogy is a statement in which two terms are related to each other in the same way as the other two terms. On the MAT, you will find 120 questions that you are expected to complete in 60 minutes. One hundred of these questions count toward your official score; twenty of them are experimental items that are being "tried out" for inclusion on a future edition of the test.

Two Categories of Analogies: Content and Relationship

There are two categories of analogies that you will find on the MAT. The first category is "content"; in these analogies, you will demonstrate your knowledge in the most typical academic areas (general knowledge, humanities, language, mathematics, natural sciences, and social sciences). The second category is "relationship"; in these analogies, you will show your ability to analyze relationships among, for example: words, definitions, expressions, classifications, characterizations, attributes, sequences, cause/effect, numerical expressions and fractions, letter patterns, and homophones (among others).

Content Objectives

The majority of the questions on the MAT are words, but they may also include parts of words, symbols, and even numerical expressions. Although some of the items are drawn from general, everyday knowledge (e.g., common expressions), most of the items are used to determine your knowledge of different academic areas. These include: humanities, language, mathematics, natural science, and social science.

Review of Analogies Found on the MAT

Humanities

Analogies on the MAT in the area of humanities can include subject matter from a wide variety of topics, including: arts, history, literature, music, philosophy, and more. These types of analogies employ a number of types of relationships. The most common ones, however, are creator/creation (e.g. composer/composition, artist/work) and whole/part (e.g., symphony/movement).

Following are areas that may be covered on the MAT, along with some sample analogies.

Art and Art History

Art history is the academic study of the history and development of the visual arts – especially considering genre, design, format, and style. This is a broad category, so let's consider what types of questions might be found in regards to art history.

The first type of art history analogy might include vocabulary from the areas of art and architecture. Knowing terms like *atrium, fresco, hieroglyphs,* and *perspective,* along with what they mean, will allow for ease of solving some art history analogies.

The second type of art history analogy may include famous artists and architects and their works. Consider brushing up on your knowledge of commonly known figures like Leonardo da Vinci, Edgar Degas, Henri Matisse, Frank Lloyd Wright, and Claude Monet and the works for which they are famous.

The third type of art and architecture analogies that you might find on the MAT involve artistic movements. Become familiar with concepts like *cubism, Gothic style, High Renaissance, impressionism,* and *realism.*

> Example:
> thespian : script :: painter: (a. volume b. palette c. lyre d. protractor)
>
> Answer: Choice (B) is correct. A thespian is an actor, typically in the theater, so he/she would use a script in order to produce their art. A painter uses a palette to hold paints while he produces his work of art.

Example:
Starry Night: Van Gogh:: *Birth of Venus::* (a. da Vinci b. Degas c. Monet d. Botticelli)

Answer: Choice (D) is correct. *Starry Night* was painted by Van Gogh. The *Birth of Venus* was painted by Botticelli.

Comparative Religion

Comparative religion is a field of study in which the growth and influence of various religions are compared, classified, and studied.

The first type of analogy you might find under this category involves the primary religions on the world and the gods that are represented by them. For example, you should know that in Islam, Allah is the creator of the universe, and in Judaism, Jehovah is the creator of the universe.

A second type of analogy under the category of religion is the most significant figures that are present within main world religions. For example, in Judaism, you might know who Solomon and Abraham were and what they did. In Confucianism, you should know who Confucius was and what he did.

You might know other things about world religions as well, including their most holy cities and locations, the festivals and holy days celebrated within them, and the main writings that guide followers of the different religions.

Example:
Hinduism: Bhrama :: Christendom: (a. God b. Jehovah c. Allah d. Shiva)

Answer: Choice (A) is correct. In Hinduism, Bhrama is the creator of life. In Christendom, God is also the creator of life.

History

This is the branch of knowledge that deals with events of the past. On the MAT, you will be expected to have some general knowledge of American history, government, and world history.

There are several categories of information that fall under the category of history. The first one involves knowing explorers and what they discovered. Familiarize yourself with people like Jacques Cartier, Sir Francis Drake, Sir Edmund Hillary, and Juan Ponce de Leon.

The second category involves significant historical figures. It is difficult to narrow this list, but consider primarily commonly known people from history – from the 1400s to current times. Examples include Martin Luther, Joan of Arc, Peter the Great, Mohatma Gandhi, and Fidel Castro.

A third area of history to consider is wars and battles that have been fought. Some examples are the Seven Years' war, the War of the Roses, and the two World Wars.

You may also encounter historical terms that require your understanding. Terms like *abolitionism, the Bill of Rights,* and *Manifest Destiny* may appear on the exam. Additionally, you might find inventors and their inventions/discoveries (e.g., Thomas Edison/light bulb, Isaac Newton/laws of motion) and American presidents.

Example:
Louis XIV: France:: Henry VII: (a. Spain b. Canada c. Italy d. England)

Answer: Choice (D) is correct. In this example, Louis XIV was the ruler of France. So, the relationship is the country of birth of the people in the analogies. The only one that is correctly written is (D); Henry VIII was king of England in the 1500s.

Literature

Literature refers to the body of artistic writings from a particular geographic area of a particular time period; these works are characterized by beauty of expression, form, and universal intellectual or emotional appeal.

Begin your approach on possible literature analogies by studying important literary figures and the major works for which they are responsible. It might help to review them by period – early history, Middle Ages, Renaissance, Romantic, Modernism, etc. Also, consider studying Greek and Roman mythology, as there are typically a couple of questions that involve that area.

Another important category of analogies that fall under the umbrella of literature is literary vocabulary. Familiarize yourself with terms like *antagonist, couplet, hyperbole,* and *paradox* to ensure that you will be able to complete these analogies.

Example:
Aphrodite: Love:: Hades: (a. war   b. pleasure   c. travelers   d. underworld)

Answer: Choice (D) is correct. Aphrodite was the Goddess of love. Hades was the god of the underworld. The other choices are incorrect, as Apollo was not the god of war (Ares was); Demeter was not the goddess of pleasure, but of the earth and underworld; Poseidon was the god of the sea.

Example:
Rime of the Ancient Mariner : Samuel Taylor Coleridge :: *Great Expectations* : (a. Robert Browning   b. Charles Dickens   c. T.S. Eliot   d. J.D. Salinger)

Answer: Choice (B) is correct. Samuel Taylor Coleridge was the author of *Rime of the Ancient Mariner*. Charles Dickens was the author of *Great Expectations*.

Modern and Classical Languages

Many people contend that an excellent education cannot be attained without the study of classical languages – a "classic education". On the MAT, this area involves particularly the study of Greek and Latin roots and their influence on modern English language.

One way to go about preparing for analogies of this type is to develop and study a list of common Greek and Latin phrases and what they mean. Another strategy is to study Greek and Latin roots, prefixes, and suffixes.

Example:

caveat emptor : buyer:: *vox populi* (a. people   b. army   c. juror   d. school)

Answer: Choice (A) is correct. The term *caveat emptor* means 'let the buyer beware'. The relationship between this pair is whom the phrase is referring to. In choice (A), *vox populi* means 'voice of the people'.

Example:

enfant terrible: ill-behaved child :: *ex cathedra* : (a. false step   b. absolute authority   c. at first glance   d. forbidden)

Answer: Choice (B) is correct. The term *enfant terrible* refers to a child that is poorly behaved. So, for the second half of the analogy, simply determine what the second term means. *Ex cathedra* means to have unquestioned or absolute authority, so that is the correct choice.

Philosophy

Philosophy is concerned with exploring the significance of beliefs or problems – primarily those dealing with reality, existence, knowledge, and values - by means of systematic, rational arguments. Philosophy is concerned with the structure of reality, the resources and limits of knowledge, the principles of moral judgment, and the relationship between language and reality.

There are two areas to study in regards to the topic of philosophy: famous philosophers and philosophy vocabulary.

Example:
Kant: morals:: Dewey: (a. education   b. economics   c. science   d. politics)

Answer: Choice (A) is correct. Immanuel Kant focused his philosophical studies in the area of moral principles. Dewey focused his philosophical studies in the area of education.

Example:
Empiricism: all knowledge comes from experience :: rationalism : (a. all knowledge comes from ideas   b. all knowledge comes from reason alone   c. all knowledge comes from learning about the external world   d. all knowledge comes from cognitive thought)

Answer: Choice (B) is correct. Empiricism suggests that all knowledge one gains comes from experiences. Rationalism suggests that all knowledge comes from reason alone.

Music

Music is the art that expresses ideas and emotions through rhythm, melody, and harmony. On the MAT, you may encounter analogies that address several different components of the music category.

First, study musical vocabulary. Knowing terms like *a capella*, staccato, octave, and *allegro* will allow you to solve many of the music analogies.

Then, study the most commonly known musicians and composers. Examples include: Johann Sebastian Bach, Aaron Copland, Duke Ellington, Felix Mendelssohn, Wolfgang Mozart, and Antonio Vivaldi.

> Example:
> crescendo : diminuendo :: piano (a. lento   b. grave   c. forte   d. contralto)
>
> Answer: Choice (C) is correct. Crescendo means to gradually become louder and diminuendo means to gradually become softer, so those words are antonyms. The antonym for piano (softly) is forte (loudly).
>
> Example:
> Baroque : Classical :: Classical : (a. Renaissance   b. Romanesque   c. Medieval d. Romantic)
>
> Answer: Choice (D) is correct. In music, the Baroque period was before the Classical period. Likewise, the Classical period came before the Romantic period – thus, choice D.

Language

This area of analogies on the MAT is specifically related to English grammar, usage, and word meanings. These test your ability to recognize relationships between those meanings.

Composition and rhetoric. Composition and rhetoric involve the art of specialized literary uses of language in prose or verse. Knowing the types of literary tools that authors use will help you be successful with this type of analogy.

Example:
Peter Piper: alliteration::crash: (a. paradox b. simile c. onomatopoeia d. hyperbole)

Answer: Choice (C) is correct. The words "Peter Piper" is an example of alliteration (repetition of consonant sounds in a line of prose). The word "crash" is an example of onomatopoeia (a word that stands for an audible sound).

Grammar. Grammar is the area of linguistics that is concerned with syntax, morphology, phonology, and semantics. On the MAT, you might find grammar analogies that address plurals, parts of speech, and the like.

Example:
millennium : millennia :: alumna (a. alumnae b. alum c. alumnus d. alumnas)

Answer: Choice (A) is correct. Millennia is the plural form of millennium, so look for a pair in which the second term is the plural form of the first. Alumnae is the plural form of alumna, so (A) is the best choice.

Word connotations

Connotations have to do with the secondary meaning of a word or expression in addition to its primary meaning. It may be a cultural or emotional attachment to a particular word, beyond its literal or explicit meaning.

Example:
Youthful: childish :: conversational : (a. talking b. chatty c. interesting d. talkative)

Answer: Choice (B) is correct. Youthful is a positive term, while childish, although a similar word, has a negative connotation. Conversational is a positive term, while chatty, a synonym, has a negative connotation.

Word meanings

This is a broad category that addresses the definitions of words and what words mean. Studying lists of commonly tested vocabulary words as well as Greek and Latin roots, prefixes, and suffixes will be helpful in solving these analogies.

Example:
regicide : king :: tyrannicide : (a. animal b. grandparent c. despot d. president)

Answer: Choice (C) is correct. In the first half of the analogy, the word regicide means the killing of a king. Therefore, choose the answer choice in which the first word is the term for the killing of the entity named in the second term.
Tyrannicide is the killing of a tyrant, dictator, or despot, so that is the correct answer.

Word parts

Word parts involve the morphology of words – prefixes, root words, suffixes.

<u>Example:</u>
bicentennial : 200 :: sesquicentennial (a. 25   b. 150   c. 50   d. 1)

Answer: Choice (B) is correct. Bicentennial means occurring every 200 years. Sesquicentennial refers to something that occurs every 150 years, so choice (B) is correct.

Mathematics

Some of the analogies on the MAT will include mathematical relationships. Analogies on the MAT may involve your knowledge of mathematical operations, relationships between different numbers and symbols, and your general knowledge of mathematics information.

Algebra

Algebra is an area of mathematics in which operations and relationships are characterized by using symbols to represent unknown numbers. In algebra analogies, you may be asked to consider numerical patterns, equations and inequalities, expressions involving absolute value and the order of operations, and scientific notation, among other topics.

> Example:
> 5 : 25 :: -6 : (a. 36   b. -36   c. 12   d. -12)
>
> Answer: Choice (A) is correct. In the stem, consider that 5 squared is 25. Negative six squared is 36.

Arithmetic

Arithmetic involves mathematical calculations – addition, subtraction, multiplication, and division. You may be asked to consider different number systems, place value, decimals, percent, and fractions.

> Example:
> 2^3 : 2^4 :: 8 : (a. 8   b. 12   c. 14   d. 16)
>
> Answer: Choice (D) is correct. $2^3 = 8$; $2^4 = 16$.

Geometry

Geometry is the branch of mathematics that deals with the properties, relationships, and measurement of lines, points, shapes, curves, and figures. On the MAT, you may be asked to solve analogies that involve the perimeter, area, and volume of figures, the distance formula, and the Pythagorean theorem.

Example:
(a. octagon   b. circle   c. triangle   d. square   ) : rectangle :: $4l : 2l + 2w$

Answer: Choice (D) is correct. To find the perimeter of a rectangle, use the formula $2l + 2w$. To find the perimeter of a square, use the formula $4l$.

Numbers. This category involves mathematical processes, as well as the relationships between numbers and types of numbers. Also, review the metric system (tip: knowing the prefixes and their meanings and the basic units of measurement – meter, liter, and gram – is helpful).

Example:
X : 10 :: D : (a. 50   b. 100   c. 500   d. 1000)

Answer: Choice (C) is correct. The Roman numeral X stands for the Arabic numeral 10. The Roman numeral D stands for the Arabic numeral 500.

Probability
Probability is the area of mathematics in which one measures the degree of confidence that one has in the occurrence of an event. Be sure that you understand basics of probability – like the difference between population and sample and the independence of events.

Example:
likely : certain :: unlikely : (a. possible   b. impossible   c. possible   d. always)

Answer: Choice (B) is correct. In this analogy, the first half signals a positive probability, from a moderate degree to a complete degree. In the second half, unlikely indicates a negative probability to a moderate degree. A negative probability to a complete degree is impossible, choice B.

Statistics

Statistics is a science that involves the collection, classification, analysis, and interpretation of numerical data. To prepare for the MAT, you might study different types of graphs that can be used to display data, along with concepts like mean, median, mode, and range.

Example:

Mode : most frequently occurring :: mean : (a. highest to lowest b. average c. value in the middle   d. statistically significant)

Answer: Choice (B) is correct. The mode is the most frequently occurring value in a group of numbers. The mean is the average of a group of numbers.

Natural Sciences

The natural sciences involve the study of nature, the physical world, and its phenomena. The MAT contains both biological and physical science analogies. The most common relationships demonstrated by the analogies include agent/object (e.g., botanist: plants) and category (e.g., carbon: element).

Astronomy

Astronomy is the branch of science that deals with the study of the universe and its bodies. It might be helpful to study different types of bodies that are found in the universe (e.g. planets, stars, comets, nebulas) and learn basic facts about them.

Example:
Nebula : (a. north star   b. crab   c. black hole   d. cloud) :: constellation: Ursa Major

Answer: Choice (B) is correct. The crab is the name of a specific nebula. Ursa Major is the name of a specific constellation.

Biology

Biology is the study of living organisms. It includes the study of their structure, function, evolution, and interrelationships. To prepare for the MAT, you might study the classification of living things, the terms used for animal young, gender, and groups, types of animal tissues, etc.

Example:
Fawn : deer :: (a. pup   b. kit   c. kid   d. calf) : seal

Answer: Choice (A) is correct. A fawn is a baby deer. A pup is a baby seal.

Chemistry

Chemistry is the branch of physical science that involves the study of substances and elements and their compositions and properties.

Example:
Carbon : C :: Iron : (a. Ir   b. Fe   c. In   d. Ni)

Answer: Choice (B) is correct. On the periodic table of elements, carbon's symbol is C. Iron's symbol is Fe.

Earth Science

Earth science is the branch of science that deals with the earth and its composition. Formally speaking, earth science could include just about anything related to the earth and its formation – geology, geography, soil science, atmospheric science, and the like.

Example:
Ocean : basalt :: crust : (a. granite   b. cobalt   c. ozone   d. igneous)

Answer: Choice (D) is correct. Basalt rock is primarily found on ocean floors. Igneous rock is found primarily in the earth's crust.

Ecology

Ecology is the study of the relationship among living things and between living things and their environments.

Example:
Smog : pollution :: Water : (a. congestion   b. erosion   c. solution   d. acidic)

Answer: Choice (B) is correct. This is a cause/effect analogy. In the first part, smog causes pollution. In the second part, water causes erosion.

Environmental Science

Environmental science deals with the physical, chemical, and biological conditions of the environment, and the effect that those things have on living things.

Example:

0° : Celsius :: (a. 212° b. 32° c. 0° d. - 100°) : Fahrenheit

Answer: Choice (B) is correct. In the metric system, 0° Celsius denotes freezing. In the standard system, 32° Fahrehneit denotes freezing.

Geology. Geology is the branch of science that is concerned with the physical history of the earth. This includes physical, chemical, and biological changes that have occurred in the past and those that are currently ongoing.

Example:

Cenozoic : Paleocene :: Triassic : (a. Silurian b. Cambrian c. Mesozoic d. Devonian)

Answer: Choice (C) is correct. The Cenozoic period marked the beginning of the Paleocene era. The Triassic period marked the beginning of the Mesozoic Era.

Physics

Physics is the area of science that deals with energy, motion, forces, and matter.

Example:

Energy : joule :: force : (a. pounds b. meter c. mass d. newton)

Answer: Choice (D) is correct. A joule is a measurement of energy. A newton is a measure of force.

Social Sciences

Social science is the study of society and the relationships of individual members within society. It includes a variety of areas, including anthropology, civics, economics, geography, political science, psychology, and sociology.

Anthropology

Anthropology is the area of social science that is concerned with the origins of humans. This includes physical development, culture, biological characteristics, and social customs.

> Example:
> androphobe : (a. germs   b. animals   c. man   d. homosexuals) :: gynophobe : woman.

> Answer: Choice (C) is correct. Androphobes fear men, as gynophobes fear women.

Civics

Civics is the area of social science that is concerned with the rights and responsibilities of citizenship.

> Example:
> president : governor :: pardon : (a. clemency   b. Republican   c. national   d. autocracy)

> Answer: Choice (A) is correct. A president may offer a pardon to someone who has been convicted of a crime, and a governor may grant clemency to the same.

Economics

Economics is a social science that is concerned with the production, distribution, and consumption of goods and services.

Example:

A certificate reflecting ownership of a corporation : stock :: a certificate reflecting a firm's promise to pay the holder a fixed sum upon maturity : (a. capital   b. bond   c. certificate of deposit   d. lien)

Answer: Choice (B) is correct. A certificate that reflects ownership in a corporation is a stock. A certificate that shows a firm's promise to pay the holder a fixed sum upon maturity (and sometimes interest payments periodically) is a bond.

Geography. Geography involves the study of the earth. This may include topics such as climate, elevation, soil, vegetation, land formations, and population.

Example:

Alps : Matterhorn :: Himalayas : (a. Montserrat   b. Athos   c. Mount McKinley   d. Mount Everest)

Answer: Choice (D) is correct. In the Alps, the highest peak is the Matternhorn. In the Himalayas, the highest peak is Mount Everest.

Political Science

Political science is the area of social science that is concerned with political institutions and the principles of government.

Example:

Kennedy: Johnson :: Eisenhower : (a. Ford   b. Kissinger   c. Humphrey   d. Nixon)

Answer: Choice (D) is correct. Johnson was Kennedy's vice president, and Nixon was Eisenhower's vice president.

Psychology

Psychology is the area of social science that deals with the mind, mental processes, and mental states in human beings.

Example:

Maslow: hierarchy of needs :: Bandura : (a. Social Learning Theory   b. Psychoanalysis   c. Theory of Psychosocial Development   d. IQ testing)

Answer: Choice (A) is correct. Maslow's contribution to psychology was his theory of the hierarchy of needs. Bandura's contribution to psychology was his Social Learning Theory.

Sociology

Sociology is the study of human society. This includes the origin, development, organization, and functioning of social relations and institutions.

Example:

Positivism: studying sociology through empirical methods :: (a. empiricism   b. mixed methods   c. functionalism   d. anti-positivism) : studying sociology through subjective perspectives.

Answer: Choice (D) is correct. Positivists recommend studying sociology empirically, similar to the way natural sciences are studied. Anti-positivists recommend studying sociology by concentrating on human cultural norms, values, symbols, and social processes, using a subjective lens.

General knowledge

This category can also be construed as "other". These items may contain information that was not covered in the other categories, and it involves things that you have learned from diverse sources. This category contains the general kinds of knowledge that an educated person might be expected to know.

Example:
Basketball : 5 :: Football : (a. 7 b. 10 c. 11 d. 13)

Answer: Choice (C) is correct. A basketball team is composed of 5 players; a football team is composed of 11 players.

Example:
New Hampshire: NH :: (a. Mississippi b. Missouri c. Montana d. Minnesota) : MO

Answer: Choice (B) is correct. New Hampshire's postal abbreviation is NH, just as Missouri's postal abbreviation is MO.

Example:
Notre Dame: South Bend :: Fordham : (a. Phoenix b. Chicago c. Washington DC d. New York City)

Answer: Choice (D) is correct. Notre Dame is a university in South Bend, Indiana as Fordham is a university in New York City.

Relationship Objectives

A number of relationship objectives are contained on the MAT. With these types of analogies, you must determine the relationship between the words and complete the analogy with the correct choice. There are several types of analogies that relate to types of connections. They include: semantic, classification, and association.

Semantic

The semantic relationship type is one that explores words. This may involve synonyms, antonyms, intensity, and word parts/meanings. To excel in semantic questions, it would be beneficial to study upper-level vocabulary words – words that are commonly tested. Another strategy is to study word parts – particularly prefixes, suffixes, and roots words. Knowing what those different parts mean can often help with decoding the meaning of a word, even if the word is unfamiliar. A final strategy is to study common words and phrases that are in foreign languages (for example, *carpe diem*, *status quo*, and *savoir-faire*).

Similarity/Contrast

Most often, similarities and contrasts involve synonyms (words that mean the same thing) or antonyms (words that have opposite meanings). An analogy that involves synonyms is primarily a definition of terms – determining one word that could be replaced with another word. In such a relationship, you must ascertain what a word means and how it is connected to the others in the analogy. An analogy that involves contrasts shows the relationship between a word and its opposite.

Example:
zenith : summit :: vale (a. nadir   b. yang   c. arboreal   d. gorge)

Answer: Choice (D) is correct. Zenith and summit are both words that refer to the highest point of something, like a mountaintop. Therefore, look for the pair of words that are synonyms. Vale and gorge both refer to low points – synonyms – so choice D is best.

brazen : clandestine :: spontaneous : (a. planned   b. desirous   c. lascivious required)

Answer: Choice (A) is correct. Brazen means obvious, and clandestine means secretive, so look for the answer choice that contains antonyms. All of the answer choices are synonyms except choice (A). Spontaneous means on the spur-of-the-moment or unplanned, so choice (A) is correct.

Intensity

An analogy that describes intensity simply compares one condition with another that has a greater or lesser degree of intensity. For example, someone might ask how you are feeling, and you might say "fine". The next time, you might say "outstanding!". Outstanding has a higher degree of intensity than simply fine.

Example:
Arctic: Pacific :: Vatican City : (a. Mexico City   b. China   c. North America   d. Russia)

Answer: Choice (D) is correct. The Arctic Ocean is the smallest ocean on Earth and the Pacific Ocean is the largest one. The Vatican City is the smallest country on Earth and Russia is the largest one.

Example:
Annoy : enrage :: enlarge : (a. decrease   b. reduce   c. exaggerate   d. increase)

Answer: Choice (C) is correct. Annoy and enrage and similar, but enrage indicates a higher intensity of that negative feeling. In the second half of the analogy, enlarge and exaggerate are similar, with the word 'exaggerate' showing a higher intensity.

Word parts and meanings

This type of analogy describes the function of another word. Often, these analogies are characterized by word parts such as prefixes and suffixes.

Example:

Ante- : before :: para- : (a. toward   b. beside   c. among   d. against)

Answer: Choice (B) is correct. The prefix para- means "beside", as evidenced in a word like parallel).

Example:

Poly- many :: semi- : (a. one   b. after   c. half   d. between)

Answer: Choice (C) is correct. The prefix semi- means "half", as evidenced in a word like semicircle or semiannual.

Classification

Classification analogies involve primarily hierarchical relationships – how one word or concept denotes a segment or an entire unit, for example. Classification analogies on the MAT are typically characterized as whole-part/part-whole, membership, and object/characteristic.

Whole-Part/Part-Whole

This type of analogy denotes the relationship between a whole thing (house, for example) and a part of the whole (room).

Example:
autocracy : individual :: meritocracy : (a. unwise b. talented c. multitude d. indigent)

Answer: Choice (B) is correct. An autocracy is a system in which one individual is rewarded with power. Therefore, look for the answer choice in which the second word is the most important part of the first word. In a meritocracy, distribution of power is based on people's ability and talent.

Membership

A membership analogy is very similar to the whole-part analogy. It shows the relationship between a whole group and a member of the group.

Example:
xenophile : foreign :: (a. hippophile b. bibliophile c. anglophile d. oenophile) : wine

Answer: Choice (D) is correct. A xenophile is a person who is interested in foreign cultures, and an oenophile is a person who is interested in wine.

Object/Characteristic

In this type of analogy, you must establish the relationship between a person or object and its characteristic.

Example:

carnivore : lion :: piscivore : (a. tiger   b. penguin   c. reptile   d. beetle)

Answer: Choice (B) is correct. A lion is a carnivore, which means it is a meat-eater. Therefore, the relationship between the two words is categorical – lions are a type of carnivore. Choice (B) is correct, because penguins are piscivores, or fish-eating.

Association

This type of analogy is the largest group that occurs on the MAT. It contains the relationship between two different, yet related concepts.

Cause/Effect

This type of analogy involves analyzing the relationship between a word and the outcome or result it causes. Occasionally, the analogy may be written with the effect first, and you must determine the cause.

> Example:
> sycophant : flatters :: raconteur : (a. critiques   b. repels   c. regales   d. leads)
>
> Answer: Choice (C) is correct. In the initial part of the analogy, a sycophant is a person who flatters others. So, in the answer choices, look for the pair in which the second word describes the effect of the first term's behavior. A raconteur is a storyteller – one who regales others with tales.

Agent/Object

This analogy type is one that shows the relationship between a person and a tool or object that he/she uses. You might also see similar analogies that involve a non-living thing – an object – and how it is used.

> Example:
> codicil : supplement :: condiment : (a. assault   b. pronounce   c. revere   d. flavor)
>
> Answer: Choice (D) is correct. A codicil is an appendix to a will; its function is to supplement or explain further. Therefore, look for the answer choice in which the second term describes the function of the first term. The purpose of condiments is to flavor food. Therefore, choice (D) is correct.

Order

In order analogies, the words are related by sequence or in a reciprocal (or opposite) circumstance.

<u>Example:</u>

Alpha ; omega :: Delaware : (a. Oregon   b. Florida   c. Maine   d. Hawaii)

Choice (D) is correct. Alpha is the first letter of the Greek alphabet and omega is the last letter. Delaware was the first state admitted to the union, and Hawaii was the last state admitted.

MAT Practice Test Questions

1.   judicious : prudent :: noxious :
        a. fruitless
        b. injurious
        c. inferior
        d. sensible

   Answer: B.

2.   fait accompli : completed :: bona fide :
        a. perfunctory
        b. indigenous
        c. general
        d. genuine

   Answer: D.

3.   carat : weight :: fathom :
        a. capacity
        b. perspective
        c. mass
        d. depth

   Answer: D.

4.   mollify : enrage :: quell :
        a. exonerate
        b. bifurcate
        c. incite
        d. denounce

   Answer: C.

5.   leonine : lion ::_____ : monkey
            a. ligneous
            b. simian
            c. feline
            d. porcine
Answer: B.

6.   cynophobia : dogs :: hemaphobia :
            a. blood
            b. deep water
            c. people
            d. mice

Answer: A.

7.   Louis Armstrong: Miles Davis :: Scott Joplin :
            a. Dizzie Gillespie
            b. Aaron Copland
            c. Benny Goodman
            d. Count Basie

Answer: D

8.   Hexagon :_____ :: 6 : 7
            a. octagon
             b. septagon
            c. nonagon
            d. dodecahedron

Answer: B.

9.   Electron :_____:: satellite : planet
          a. proton
          b. nucleus
          c. atom
          d. neutron
       Answer: B.

10.   Habitat : location :: _____ : role
          a. capacity
          b. competition
          c. niche
          d. predation

       Answer: C.

11.   Blue: base :: red :
          a. acid
           b. saline
          c. alkaline
          d. element

       Answer: A

12.   Handel : baroque :: Mozart
a. romantic
b. operatic
c. modern
d. classical

       Answer: D

13.   26 : even :: _____ : prime
              a. 8
              b. 11
              c. 15
              d. 20

       Answer: B.

14.   Cytology : cells :: _____ : fungi
              a. mycology
              b. ornithology
              c. oncology
              d. phrenology
       Answer: A

15.   Darwin : evolution :: Mendel :
              a. blood groups
               b. popular culture
              c. relative dating
              d. genetics

       Answer: D.

16.   *Sense and Sensibility:* Jane Austen :: *Wuthering Heights* :
              a. Charles Dickens
              b. Mary Shelley
              c. Emily Bronte
              d. Henry David Thoreau

       Answer: C.

17.   Gustave Eiffel : Eiffel Tower :: _____ : Monticello
        a. Henry Bacon
        b. Frank Lloyd Wright
        c. Jackson Pollack
        d. Thomas Jefferson

        Answer: D.

18.   Neil Armstrong: first man to walk on the moon :: _____: first Englishman
        to circumnavigate the earth.
        a. Sir Edmund Hillary
        b. Sir Francis Drake
        c. Christopher Columbus
        d. Prince Henry the Navigator
        Answer: B.

19.   Thirty Years War : 30 :: Hundred Years War :
        a. 60 years
        b. 100 years
        c. 116 years
        d. 52 years

        Answer: C.

20.   Catherine the Great : Latvia :: Napoleon :
        a. Paris
        b. Elba
        c. Waterloo
        d. Corsica

        Answer: C.

21.   apparition : translucent :: tumbler :
        a. transparent
        b. dingy
        c. emaciated
        d. grandiose

        Answer: A

22.   Sacramento : California :: _____ : Florida
        a. Orlando
        b. Tallahassee
        c. Miami
        d. Jacksonville

        Answer: B

23.   appease : placate :: obviate :
        a. disregard
        b. clarify
        c. decide
        d. preclude

        Answer: D

24.   Plato : *Republic* :: Virgil :
        a. *Odysseus*
        b. *Iliad*
        c. *The Aeneid*
        d. *Helen of Troy*

        Answer: C

25.   Gustav Eiffel : Eiffel Tower :: Henry Bacon :
        a. Lincoln Memorial
        b. Statue of Liberty
        c. The White House
        d. the Sears Tower

Answer: A.

26.   Cortez : Mexico :: Cartier :
        a. North America
        b. Canada
        c. East Indies
        d. Florida

Answer: B.

27.   Kierkegaard : existentialism :: Husserl :
        a. empiricism
        b. idealism
        c. positivism
        d. phenomenology

Answer: D

28.   chicken : brood :: cats :
        a. clowder
        b. herd
        c. swarm
        d. army

Answer: A

29.   _____: Missouri :: Granite : New Hampshire
        a. Tar Heel
        b. Sunshine
        c. Show Me
        d. Buckeye
   Answer: C

30.   Justinian : Byzantium :: Augustus :
        a. Macedonia
        b. Rome
        c. Athens
        d. Sparta

   Answer: B

31.   latitude : longitude :: parallels :
        a. lines
        b. equator
        c. degrees
        d. meridians

   Answer: D

32.   anemometer : wind speed : sphygmomanometer : _____
        a. weight
        b. atmospheric pressure
        c. distance
        d. blood pressure

   Answer: D

33.   Michelangelo : Buonarroti : Rembrandt : _____

        a. Van Rijn

        b. Degas

        c. Donaluce

        d. Van Vleet

        Answer: A

34.   *Gulliver's Travels* : Jonathan Swift :: *Frankenstein* : _____

        a. John Keats

        b. George Eliot

        c. Mary Shelley

        d. Alexander Pope

        Answer: C.

35.   *David* : Michelangelo :: *The Thinker* : _____

        a. Claude Monet

        b. Auguste Rodin

        c. Vincent Van Gogh

        d. Henry Moore

        Answer: B

36.   da Gama : Portugal :: Cabot : _____

        a. France

        b. Belgium

        c. New Zealand

        d. Italy

        Answer: D

37.   Artemis : Diana :: Aphrodite : _____
        a. Venus
        b. Demeter
        c. Hera
        d. Pandora

Answer: A

38.   carbon : 6 :: hydrogen : _____
        a. 1
        b. 2
        c. 3
        d. 4

Answer: A

39.   newton : force :: _____ : power
        a. joule
        b. tesla
        c. watt
        d. hertz
Answer: C

40.   0° latitude : equator :: 23.5° south latitude : _____
        a. prime meridian
        b. tropic of Capricorn
        c. middle latitude
        d. tropic of Cancer

Answer: B

41. cartographer : _____ :: entomologist : arachnologist
   a. geographer
   b. geologist
   c. archaeologist
   d. botanist

   Answer: A

42. Gold Coast : Ghana :: Barbary Coast : _____
   a. Zimbabwe
   b. Chad
   c. South Africa
   d. North Africa

   Answer: D

43. clarinet :_____ :: cello : string
   a. brass
   b. woodwind
   c. percussion
   d. horn

   Answer: B

44. John Keats : Romantic :: John Milton : _____
   a. Neoclassical
   b. Victorian
   c. post-Modernism
   d. Renaissance

   Answer: D.

45. hatching : parallel lines :: stippling : _____

      a. squares

      b. dots

      c. perpendicular lines

      d. curves

Answer: B

46. Bill Clinton : NAFTA :: Jimmie Carter : _____

      a. Peace Corps

      b. Medicare

      c. Department of Education

      d. New Deal coalition

Answer: C

47. Theseus : minotaur :: Perseus : _____

      a. Medusa

      b. the Muses

      c. Menelaus

      d. the Tritons

Answer: A

48. capacity : liter :: mass : _____

      a. meter

      b. kilometer

      c. gram

      d. pound

Answer: C

49.   inaugurate: President :: coronate : _____
           a. pope
           b. cardinal
           c. bishop
           d. monarch

       Answer: D

50.   George W. Bush : Bill Clinton :: Augustus : _____
           a. Claudine
           b. Gaius
           c. Tiberius
           d. Antony

       Answer: C

51.   positive : negative ::_____ : flat
           a. sharp
           b. tone
           c. bass
           d. treble

       Answer: A

52.   tibia : fibula : ulna : _____
a. sternum
b. radius
c. femur
d. ankle

       Answer: B

53.   Zn : zinc :: Ag : _____
          a. iron
          b. silver
          c. sodium
          d. arsenic

        Answer: B

54.   *Because I Could Not Stop for Death* : Emily Dickinson :: *The Road Not Taken*
        :_____
          a. Elizabeth Barrett Browning
          b. Robert Frost
          c. William Shakespeare
          d. William Wordsworth

        Answer: B

55.   Fugue: polyphonic :: _____: monophonic
          a. Gregorian chant
          b. mass
          c. recitation
          d. madrigal
        Answer: A

56.   bourgeoisie : _____ :: Proletariat : laboring class
          a. upper class
          b. ruling class
          c. middle class
          d. poor
        Answer: C

57.   Poseidon : sea :: _____ : war
           a. Hades
           b. Ares
           c. Apollo
           d. Pan
       Answer: B

58.   Richard Nixon : Milhous :: Jimmy Carter : _____
           a. Wilson
           b. Baines
           c. Herbert
           d. Earl

       Answer: D

59.   Hindi : India :: _____ : Brazil
           a. Spanish
           b. English
           c. Portuguese
           d. French
       Answer: C

60.   2 : 8 :: 3 : _____
           a. 9
           b. 12
           c. 27
           d. 30

       Answer: C

61. O : oxygen :: K : _____
    a. potassium
    b. chromium
    c. nickel
    d. krypton

    Answer: A

62. Michelangelo : painter :: Frank Lloyd Wright : _____
    a. writer
    b. sculptor
    c. playwright
    d. architect

    Answer: D

63. length x width : πr^2 :: _____ : circle
    a. triangle
    b. pyramid
    c. square
    d. prism
    Answer: C

64. John Steinbeck : novelist :: Arthur Miller : _____
a. playwright
b. poet
c. essayist
d. lyricist

    Answer: A

65. *Rhapsody in Blue* : George Gershwin :: *Appalachian Spring* : _____
    a. John Coltrane
    b. Duke Ellington
    c. Aaron Copland
    d. Leonard Bernstein

    Answer: C

66. Cultural Revolution : Mao Zedong :: Reformation : _____
    a. Karl Marx
    b. Martin Luther
    c. John Calvin
    d. Thomas Moore

    Answer: B

67. Judaism : temple :: Islam : _____
    a. church
    b. synagogue
    c. mosque
    d. mecca

    Answer: C

68. 8 : 10 :: octagon : _____
    a. dodecahedron
    b. pentagon
    c. polygon
    d. decagon

    Answer: D

69.   Romeo and Juliet : tragedy :: Richard III : _____
       a. history
       b. romance
       c. comedy
       d. fantasy

       Answer: A

70.   Communism : Marx :: _____ : Mussolini
       a. Nazism
       b. fascism
       c. nationalism
       d. socialism
       Answer: B

71.   Mozart : 1700s :: Henry VIII : _____
       a. 1400s
       b. 1500s
       c. 1600s
       d. 1800s

       Answer: B

72.   Hockey: Stanley Cup :: _____ : Gray Cup
       a. football
       b. soccer
       c. yachting
       d. gymnastics
       Answer: A

73. Right to keep and bear arms : 2nd amendment :: right to unlawful search and seizure : _____
   a. 1st amendment
   b. 3rd amendment
   c. 4th amendment
   d. 6th amendment

   Answer: C

74. Ernest Hemingway : *The Old Man and the Sea* ::_____: *To Kill a Mockingbird*
   a. Eugene O'Neill
   b. J.D. Salinger
   c. Harper Lee
   d. Upton Sinclair
   Answer: C

75. Dizzy Gillespie : trumpet :: Charlie Parker : _____
   a. piano
   b. saxophone
   c. clarinet
   d. organ

   Answer: B

76. Eli Whitney : cotton gin :: _____ : moveable type
   a. Thomas Edison
   b. Nicolaus Copernicus
   c. Johannes Gutenberg
   d. Leonardo da Vinci
   Answer: C

77.   Entomologist : insects :: ichthyologist: _____
            a. fish
            b. spiders
            c. diseases
            d. metals
        Answer: A

78.   London : England :: _____ : Germany
            a. Munich
            b. Vienna
            c. Berlin
            d. Hamburg
        Answer: C

79.   Olivia : Antonio :: _____ : Cassius
            a. Polonius
            b. Laertes
            c. MacDuff
            d. Brutus
        Answer: D

80.   Crypto : hidden :: _____ : dance
            a. cardio
            b. choreo
            c. chrono
            d. ethno

        Answer: B

81.   verb : adverb :: noun : _____
           a. adjective
           b. pronoun
           c. preposition
           d. conjunction

       Answer: A

82.   electron : negative :: neutron : _____
           a. positive
           b. negative
           c. none
           d. proton

       Answer: C

83.   acrophobia : heights :: hydrophobia :
           a. blood
           b. water
           c. food
           d. death

       Answer: B

84.   haiku : 3 :: sonnet :
           a. 6
           b. 8
           c. 12
           d. 14

       Answer: D

85. Benny Goodman : "King of Swing" :: _____ : "Satchmo"
   a. Louis Armstrong
   b. Miles Davis
   c. Cole Porter
   d. Scott Joplin

   Answer: A

86. *Das Kapital* : Karl Marx :: *The Wealth of Nations* : _____
   a. Jeremy Bentham
   b. John Locke
   c. Adam Smith
   d. John Rawls

   Answer: C

87. bacteriologist : bacteria :: _____ : coins
   a. discophile
   b. metallurgist
   c. thanatologist
   d. numismatist

   Answer: D

88. Lincoln : John Wilkes Booth :: Reagan : _____
   a James Earl Ray
   b. John Hinkley
   c. Leon Czolgosz
   d. Charles Guiteau

   Answer: B

89. Egypt : Babylon :: pyramids : _____
    a. Hanging Gardens
    b. Colossus
    c. Great Library
    d. Taj Mahal

Answer: A

90. Hippocrates : medicine :: Euclid : _____
    a. drama
    b. sculpture
    c. astronomy
    d. geometry

Answer: D

91. scholar : erudite :: reprobate : _____
    a. scrupulous
    b. depraved
    c. peaceful
    d. whimsical

Answer: B

92. Sound : 1,088 feet per second :: Light : _____
    a. 186,000 feet per second
    b. 186,000 miles per second
    c. 1,600,000 feet per second
    d. 1,680 miles per second

Answer: B

93.   Television : Emmy :: _____ : Tony
            a. journalism
            b. Broadway theater
            c. atomic energy
            d. literature

        Answer: B

94.   ballad : _____ :: fable : story
            a. story
            b. poem
            c. drama
            d. tune

        Answer: B

95.   Tchaikovsky: *The Nutcracker* :: _____ : *The Marriage of Figaro*
            a. Vivaldi
            b. Straus
            c. Mozart
            d. Ravel

        Answer: C

96.   John Jacques Rousseau : education :: Thomas Hobbes : _____
            a. logic
            b. psychology
            c. politics
            d. theology

        Answer: C

97.   duck : drake :: bee : _____
            a. jill
            b. larva
            c. queen
            d. drone

    Answer: D

98.   Arabic : 400 :: Roman : _____
            a. MD
            b. DC
            c. CCCC
            d. CD

    Answer: D

99.   Russia : Czar :: _____ : Khan
            a. Egypt
            b. Mongolia
            c. Turkey
            d. China

    Answer: B

100.   Doric : column :: Gambrel : _____
            a. roof
            b. ceiling
            b. mantel
            c. atrium

    Answer: A

Made in the USA
Lexington, KY
09 June 2019